Dandelions in Third Space

poems
Edytta Wojnar

STEPHEN F. AUSTIN STATE UNIVERSITY PRESS

Production Manager: Kimberly Verhines
Book Design: Mallory LeCroy
Cover Art: Karina Wojnar

IBSN: 978-1-62288-236-6

For more information: Stephen F. Austin State University Press
P.O. Box 13007 SFA Station
Nacogdoches, Texas 75962
sfapress@sfasu.edu
www.sfasu.edu/sfapress
936-468-1078

Distributed by Texas A&M University Press Consortium
www.tamupress.com

Contents

A New Destination \ 9

Part One

The Immigrants \ 13

My Mother's Necklace \ 14

Lion's Tooth Ode \ 15

Balicka Street, 1981 \ 16

Coming to America \ 17

Seven Years of Plenty \ 18

The Other Side \ 19

Remembrance \ 20

Wizyta \ 21

What Flows in Our Veins \ 22

To a Foreign Language \ 24

Part Two

Homepage \ 27

Just Wait & See \ 28

A Woman \ 29

Waiting for the Results \ 30

In Nairobi \ 31

Flying Back Home \ 32

Kids & Fish Have No Voice \ 33

the day the light went out \ 34

Like a Loving Mother \ 35

Fibonacci Spiral \ 36

I Named Her Nina \ 37

i have the right to walk on my eyelashes \ 38

Tidal Wave \ 39

Curse \ 40

Weekend at Wyndham Hotel \ 41

Date Night \ 42

Throwing Stones \ 43

With Google Earth \ 44

Deconstructing Darkness: Contemplating Plath & van Gogh Alive \ 45

Synestia \ 47

Insomnia \ 48

The Art of Kissing \ 49

Newton's Law \ 50

With You \ 51

Good Life \ 52

Shadow Puppets \ 53

husband & wife \ 54

Failed Assignment \ 55

Older \ 56

To Aging Well \ 57

October \ 58

Letting Them Go \ 59

Slideshow \ 60

Doing Dishes with My Son \ 62

Visiting My Son in Japan \ 63

Keeping You Safe \ 64

Syzygy \ 65

Part Three

At a House Party \ 69

our ridiculous world \ 70

Covid-19 Guilt Poem \ 71

Global Change \ 72

Chernobyl, 26 April 1986 \ 73

The Aftermath \ 74

Enigma of Distance \ 75

"Guernica" \ 76

alternate reality \ 77

Negotiation \ 78

In the melting pot \ 79

Northern New Jersey Town \ 80

Semester Abroad in India \ 81

book of faces \ 82

Cosmic Rules \ 83

Struck \ 84

the unknown \ 85

Storm \ 86

Tattoos \ 87

Thesaurus \ 88

Ars Poetica Triptych \ 89

Acknowledgments \ 91

To Peter, Sebastian, Kristian, & Karina

Fate has been kind
to me thus far.

I might never have been given
the memory of happy moments.

~Wisława Szymborska

Try to praise the mutilated world.
Remember June's long days,
and wild strawberries, drops of rosé wine.
[…]
Praise the mutilated world
and the gray feather a thrush lost,
and the gentle light that strays and vanishes
and returns.

~Adam Zagajewski

A New Destination

taking off
requires an effort

cabin doors locked
you fastened in your seat

your hands hold onto armrests
the way you hold on to the past

but once the gravity
stops pulling

time unfolds
loses hours in the sky

you don't mind
the not knowing

between destinations
nothing out there but clouds

while engines hum
a mantra of now

the plane arches its course
& lands on the ground

that spins & tilts
but somehow feels steady to you

Part One

The Immigrants

                         on a new continent
behind cash registers
in a Key Food store   they stay silent
                                                       searching for words

their dreams   in a foreign language
                         when summoned
                         by their sons' teachers
                         they fold their tongues
flat like an ironed rag

                         The 22-year-olds   remove asbestos
                                               from boiler rooms
                         in Brooklyn
                                               their clothes in garbage bags
sealed

Their children   who speak several languages
able to translate any silence —still
                         wherever they are   a part of them always alien

My Mother's Necklace

On my neck
bursztynowy naszyjnik—
the color of butterscotch
mint, honey, soothing

my vocal cords
plucked by Germanic
words, unlike
the shushing sounds
of my mother tongue
flowing like mom's
silk scarf I lost at the prom.

I left my home country
& learned
a lie can be true—
life can be wasted
& there is a metaphor
for every loss—even language.

My voice confined
for years in the larynx
like a beetle in resin.

Lion's Tooth Ode

(Dent de lion)

Each spring, dandelions
bloom on my lawn, their tooth-like
leaves & golden heads

healing & wholesome.
Hands protected by gloves,
neighbors with hoes

pull from their backyards
roots of this alien
invasive species from Europe—

milky sap leaving stains
when the stem is broken.
Eastern & old, destined

to disappear, my people uprooted
in wars, camps, gulags.
White parachutes gliding on wind

landing on someone else's soil.

Balicka Street, 1981

Golden autumn. Zlota jesien. At this latitude
leaves touched by sunrays turn gold & linger
while whispering verses in the wind.
Chestnuts shed their spiny burrs like music notes.
The moon gives gold to everything I touch.
I am where I shouldn't be at 1 am, a boy's arms
around me. His hair, bleached from hours at a public pool,
gold even at night. We do nothing wrong.
We look up at the sky with its golden sparks.
This kind of peace should be shared
before lives are shared.
Before things go wrong & we break.
Before I forget my street lined with towers of gold
windows like stars, reflecting what was splendid.

December fog clings to my bedroom window.
Big Dipper lowers towards gray roofs.
Sparrows fly to a windowsill but do not sing.
Gray horse pulls a wagon. Horseshoes click clack.
Voice, hoarse from cigarettes, growls: *Ziemniaki*!
Cebula!!! Potatoes & onion for sale.
This kind of food fills basements before there is nothing
but bottles of vinegar & vodka for sale
& rations of flour & meat must be bought by curfew.
Before tramways halt & phones stop ringing.
Before the State of War.
Before I will remember my street
in the darkness of that winter.
Before I leave & never come back home.

Coming to America

I arrived on the night of fire, in the black sky
golden mums fuller than a full moon.

After the show, a cloud settled
on the yellow hood of a cab

as we drove from the airport
thru the back streets

of Brooklyn where the homeless
        rummaged garbage bags
                left to rot
                        in the July heat
        & teenagers
                winged with drugs
                        zigzagged
                                to fuse with darkness.

When the taxi stopped on Henry Street
tattering a corpse (a squirrel?)

my husband said tenderly,
witaj, welcome home, kochanie.

Seven Years of Plenty

"Behold, there come seven years of great plenty (...);
and there shall arise after them seven years of famine"
Genesis 41:29

Those were the good times
at a Brooklyn studio

a walkup on the top floor
160 a month including heat

full-size mattress
in a corner—white crib

"Hounds of Love" on a turntable
laundry hand washed in a tub

freezing on fire escape stairs
until dried stiff

Twin Towers still
taller than rooftop antennas

& red paper hearts
glued to the white kitchen wall.

The Other Side

I saw many from my generation
fly over the Atlantic to crawl
in basements. Pipe by pipe,

we removed asbestos
brick by brick, we built towers scraping the sky.
Watched with suspicion,

we rounded our backs. We flexed
our vocal cords to accommodate
English sounds, yet our accent stayed

guilty of always-worthless viewpoints,
the tongue-twisting names a signal to cite
one of the Polish jokes media continued to air.

We built our new lives on familiar old
blueprints our countrymen erased
back home while we were gone, socialist ethics

dismantled like the Berlin Wall,
friends we shared school desks
& stolen cigarettes with, lost.

Wherever we are, we are alien. Greying,
growing wrinkles, restless we howl
at a blue moon.

On the other side, the soil
rich with blood. Our ancestors'
tombs light the sky.

Remembrance

after Stanley Kunitz

My father cannot forgive himself
for losing his mother twice.

He remembers the day
the Russians marched in
to their village in eastern Poland
when he was six. He remembers
following a horse-drawn wagon
that carried his mother in a pine box
he click-clack of horseshoes
& the swoosh of military
worn-out boots on cobblestone.

Now my father is seventy-eight.
We visit the cemetery
where his parents rest. The wind tangles
the branches of birch trees.
We follow directions from a registrar
for war graves
but cannot find the tomb.
Marked with an "X" on the map
it must be buried
underneath weeds & vines.
It thunders. Raindrops
fall on my father's face.

Red dirt on his clothes & skin
he yanks the weeds
with hands swollen from arthritis.
Like a child he wipes
his eyes with soiled sleeves
to read the name
revealed on a plaque. *Mama,*
he cries, *Wreszcie cie znalazlem!*
I have finally found you!
& buries his face
in the muddy mound.

Wizyta

full of hope & money
we go back to hometowns   the colorful Old Towns
    with indefatigable florists
     & old college friends   under flickering lights
       snow sifts
       like powdered sugar

our backs broken
bones & hair thinning   how delicious rye bread
    crust seeded with caraway
     bought warm at a bakery   pączki—amber balls
       of sweet dough filled with
       rosehip and rum

we un-silence voices
coarse from cries & vodka   on Szewska a click clack
    of heels on cobblestone
     like keys on an accordion   memories pour
       like wine served hot
       on cold days at Camelot Café

we sip failures
& dollars we've earned   brown chestnuts
    on a blanket of snow
     like notes on music sheets   under the gold light
       of bronze streetlamps
       snowflakes are fireflies

What Flows in Our Veins

You are a frog! Zaba jestes! Lips
lost in a toothless mouth screeched
when I skipped by a bag of bones
propped against warm tiles of a coal stove.
One time, crooked fingers emerged
from beneath a dark shawl & pulled
on my neatly braided hair.

I was told my Great Grandma's mind
was broken from living too long.

In 1917 she killed her husband, she'd repeat.
Soldiers shot him against a brick wall
but it was she who hid his gun
in their baby's diaper when Germans
searched the kitchen. She didn't know
they would snatch
the crying baby from her arms.

I used to be pretty and vain, Baba
would sigh, *your grandfather carefree.*
Then bombs fell.
Blood in the gutters. A bullet
hole in a loaf of bread.
Newborns frozen in cribs.

*Baltic Sea turned to ice
& your mama cried
from hunger every night
that winter of 1941,* Grandma would say
while buttering a slice of bread for my supper.

In the end, she stopped eating.
She was tired of living.

Now, she visits me at night
to unveil the untold stories
& when I stop eating,
she whispers: *Don't be frightened.*
Walcz! Fight!

To a Foreign Language

I write my thoughts
(growing wild around the fence
sprouting thorns
& dripping sap)
down
in English
leaving links
of conjugation
delicate rules
of declension & family
expectations
behind
the borders.
These were crossed
years ago. The rules
have changed.

Part Two

Homepage

a woman dances on the beach
leaving behind a plastic pig
a wedding ring left shoe
a bottle of hot sauce
a bag of lemons one dollar bill
a sex toy more condoms
than cigarette butts a man
who barely avoided being
crushed by a FedEx truck

Just Wait & See

On Monday I've given up all
thinking about being good
while singing with Bobby "Blue" Bland
on the way to Pompton Plains.
Further on up the road I've decided
I don't have to be
loving all the time—
sometimes even loving
thoughts can take
you from yourself.

If a life becomes irrelevant
the cosmic cut will suck
the breath out of this body you wear.
It will track you down
in every life you plan to have.
That's what I have learned.
I don't plan—I am not
afraid of the unknown.

Each mystery
gets to be discovered.
For instance, the largest
spiral galaxy, bigger
than the Milky Way
has just been spotted
—after a collision
a million years ago.
Just wait & see.

A Woman

When at night her feet grew roots
& her chest split open
waking her

she stood in front of a mirror
to examine her breasts

where a new lump
sprouted under her fingers

the size of a pebble
yet it felt like a stone

thrown at her standing
in the middle of a stadium

to punish her body
for allowing a man to worship it

for baring her breasts
able to turn water
into nourishment

Waiting for the Results

For the third time, I lie on a table
to be probed & cut.

Will the cells multiply
biting into my armpit? My bones?
Will I be in pain?

What if malicious cells
attack my brain? I might not recognize
myself. I might laugh
for no reason, lose interest
in doing things I used to love.

Like loving my children.

Does a fish grow seasick from swimming?
A bird airsick from soaring?

I grow sick from worrying.
I want the life of another animal.

In Nairobi

jammed between city buses
& a herd of cows—
like a hippopotamus
hemmed in by tourists
in a mangrove swamp—
our safari van is surrounded

by begging women
who tap on windows
their open palms
leaving prints
on glass covered with red dust

their bodies mutilated
to never feel pleasure
carry babies
swaddled in shukas
on backs hunched
from daily lugging
of firewood & water

I lower my window
& thin arms—branches
of African Acacia—reach inside
to collect dollar bills
fingers quick like wind

so when Michael in the front seat
traveling from Washington DC
hollers *Jesus Christ!*
close the freaking window!
I summon upon him a visit
from female mosquitoes

& leave the window ajar.

Flying Back Home

Somewhere above Greenland
the baby falls asleep on my lap

& her brothers take turns
kicking the back of seats.

Their father will meet us
at the gate, his hair styled

by young manicured hands,
which washed & ironed his shirts.

I sensed his betrayal
before boarding the plane

yet I stay buckled.
Leaning against a cold window

I watch the white land disappear
beneath unsettled clouds.

Kids & Fish Have No Voice

Those days, kids did not talk unasked. Kids
were not asked. Years ago my children asked

for a fish tank. They named the fishes:
Beady, Raspberry, Sunny, Oopsy. Cried each time
a fish died. They still talk about the fish,

how the big ones ate the fry.
My husband will give me anything when I ask.
Once I asked & he would not give me the answer.

My in-laws say some things are better left unsaid
believing that not naming will undo the pain.
Some friends advise to name the hurt in therapy.

My mother says not to tell my father as it
would make him angry & asks if I remember
Barbara's husband who has just battled test-

icular cancer. *You would not believe the rest*
she says. At this point I will believe anything

the way I believe in no one.

the day the light went out

the day begins
like any Sunday in May   the golden sun round
                        & fierce in the sky—   a halogen
                                           bulb on a Command hook

she passes by & wives hold
onto their men's arms   she opens a window
                        & shutters shift   a halo in the mist

as if her breath spun silk
tangling a scarlet web   crumbling clouds
                        in a fury—   a cumulus swelling

her laughter
making them afraid of   wrecked words
                        eddying sadness   growing sly tentacles

lonesomeness   tied like a question   on a copper cable

Like a Loving Mother

you come to me
on rays of a rising sun,
unclench the fist my fingers form

& one by one

oil my monsters with forgiveness.
You don't have to be
perfect anymore, you whisper.

You tell me to disrobe the skin,
untangle my breath
from bones and veins—an embryo

in your womb, you tuck me in.

Fibonacci Spiral

you
said
I was
a flower
lilylike daisy
a buttercup a hurricane
your universe my uterus in the golden phi

I want to crawl into you sometimes I want
       to be hugged I hug myself

you worry about me you worry
       I'll spiral so you ask for
a
new
feeling
some people
have feelings before
& after but the trick is to
stop

circling
       a hawk approaches its prey

I Named Her Nina

The radiologist left in a hurry,
an ultrasound humming, the screen
turned at an angle I couldn't see—
my belly cold & sticky with gel.

When the doctor pointed
to the image explaining
what went wrong, I caressed
the baby I couldn't sustain.

I lost a lot of blood that Monday
at the Chilton Memorial.
Back home, bent in two
I rocked & cried.

The next day a friend called
before 9am urging to turn the TV on.
On the screen, flight 175
& the South Tower on fire.

My husband came home late
that night. His ashen hair
smelled of burnt flesh.
Nobody mentioned Nina.

i have the right to walk on my eyelashes

When it hails in July
ice the size of an eyeball   i give birth
                     to gods & heroes   a sunray twists
                                       my loosely pinned hair

i intent on doing nothing
but catching ice with my teeth i nurture my monsters
                     with nectar   ruby earrings
                                     sway to unsung notes

When the moon is a silver sliver
i unfold like a silk robe   bathe in a river
                     turning stones   & when sadness spreads
                                     its copper-colored claws

i flutter my heart & tie words
to merlot roses   i am the fog woman
                     carved in cedar   despite the promise
                                   i fall

i walk on my eyelashes
clouds at my feet   Some say
                 i have magical powers dragonfly wings & frogs
                                     leap from my hands

Tidal Wave

For decades we cradled
& hogged our oneness

surfed in unison (we thought)
our mouths full of water.

After tasting the innerness
of the other
we gasped twisting
into sea fire
our glassy eyes blaming.

We drowned
with bellies full of mud

the waning moon bruised & dim.

Curse

May a nicotine haze
wrinkle your face into a dry leaf
maggots eat

May cellulite like spiced latte
spill on your thighs & your
sagging breasts

May remorse the size of Pangea
remain in your chest
for 100 million years

May you miss him

while he minces the fossils
of whatever
you think you've had

May my curse
mutate into forgiveness—
a songless blackbird

Weekend at Wyndham Hotel

Just once
I want to be a danger
to your stubborn love. I want
to have one secret, a clever lie
with an alibi. I want
to be kissed by a stranger
in a hotel elevator, untie
his tie, unbutton a collar
unbuckle, unzip, just once
I want to look with wildness
into not-your-blue eyes. I want
to be a danger to your contentment
& confident plans.
                                At Wyndham
on the way to the fifth floor
he stares at my breasts
unties my blouse with his eyes
smiles & bites
the inside of his cheek then holds
the elevator door open while I slide
a plastic key in the lock of room 513
& shut the door behind me without
looking back. Panicked, I reach
for the phone. It buzzes
in my purse with a text from you.
Just once I want to be a danger.

Date Night

On the E train, I listen to Dire
Straits' *Making Movies*, the album's red
cover flashing under my eyelids
while I hum "Tunnel of Love."
By the time "Expresso Love" is on its last note,
I swallow the aftertaste,
but the bitterness won't leave
my body while my feet navigate
the subway's tiled tunnels
exiting at the corner of Fifth & 53rd—
my husband in a crisply ironed
shirt that matches the silver
on his temples, waiting
for someone who used to be
crazy for him.

Throwing Stones

We choose an unmarked trail leading
to a lake. You cup my hand in yours & keep it
warm in your pocket. When you let go
to climb a slippery boulder by the water,

I chew on my lip. I am cold & want to get back

on the trail. You gather a few stones & aim
at a black gap sparkling on the frozen lake.
First pebble slides on the ice,
the next ones disappear with a splash.

You turn around & wait for my applause.

With Google Earth

we zoom
in on Krakow
Market Place
where we used
to stroll
past curfew
kiss & caress
in the dark

& you
recall when
from a stall
you stole
a walnut
shaped like
a heart
to give me

& we
look for it
in a jewelry
box where
a red
velvet holds
an empty shell.

Deconstructing Darkness
Contemplating Plath and van Gogh Alive

after Robin Coste Lewis

Some body follows me home. On a wall, sunflowers in a vase. I like the way they stand tall unaware of their beauty, heads bowing, heavy with seeds, dark before harvest. I think of a summer day forty years ago when I offered a glass of cold water to a stranger, sun in my eyes, front door wide open. The violent crash. Still life on the ground.

teeth bite the flesh of clouds.

you bite the ear of someone you want.
oh, the crazy taste!

he slices his left ear off.
my ear cut & pinned is perfect, so I wear my hair down.

   *

why do we wallow
obsessed with light, a bullet,
carbon monoxide, the bottle of
pills we might swallow,
the water's edge.

   *

Picturing an empty wall in the living space he could claim his own, he stretches the canvas to fit a sky, blends nocturnal tides & traces foreign lands upside down.

in another   hemisphere
    I stand on my head
clouds scramble my feet

Sylvia, you cross the deepest blue but keep the language. I become mute.

*

Van Gogh swirls the stars. "Stars are dropping thick as stones," you say &
stay horizontal to converse with the sky.

*

You can look into the throat of sky but not your lover's thoughts.

"The tulips are too red," you say. You are right, their redness hurts if you
hold them close to your chest. Redness is a kind of hunger that nothing
will kill.

It's so easy to reach down to anger, lips in a straight line deflating promises
into a hiss: *this wrong will always burn the ground under your feet*. When
words like this shoot between my fingers clasped over raw rage, I'm afraid.

*

Older now, I hold on
to mornings—beams of
light under the roof of clouds
& wind rustling
the green robes of grass.

Synestia

a computer simulation shows
consistent spinning can vaporize a rock
concealing the Moon's origin

on Monday the doctor points
to a dip on my EKG revealing
I had a heart attack

could be a computer error too he says
& asks about my family or anything
that could cause stress

I reply everyone is doing great & yes
my oldest still works in Koya-san

computer images of double star stitches
don't show the real ups & downs
the sudden breaks & hard-to-breathe comebacks

so I don't mention cans of All Day IPA
my husband recycles every night

nor his father's funeral
on Saturday when no one cried

Insomnia

I don't long for it
in bed   my husband's
chiseled chin   his throat
an accordion

eyes open   I don't summon
its unrequired symmetry
high tides   and retreating
          waves

my flesh   flotsam
conspiring to become
the full moon

          a frantic
shore collecting
worries like amber

The Art of Kissing

All species kiss. To kiss is to get close
enough to smell the perfect match.
Kissing is inhaling each other's soul.

Snails caress antennae, puffins rub bills,
elephants thrust their trunks into each
others' mouths. All species kiss to get close.

In lieu of a promise some people blow
from their fingertips a kiss to catch.
Kissing is inhaling each other's soul.

Some like messy kisses that engage all
thirty four muscles, burn calories, slash
cholesterol. To kiss is to feel close.

Kiss for good luck beneath the mistletoe
but not on the lips if you need to detach!
Kissing is inhaling each other's soul.

Lips & tongues have an eternal role
(tasting sweet like blood & sugar) to snatch
a breath. The last kiss to feel close.
Kissing is inhaling each other's soul.

Newton's Law

I love you. I always want you
to love me.

I know you do
what your desire is

but then don't
rage at the results.

For every action
there is a reaction.

It's the law. You love
me, I love you back.

With You

In the backyard
among blades of tall grass
dandelions' yellow heads turn white.
Children snap hollow milky stems
then blow at the fluffy tufts
to plant pixie dust.

In the Andes
stray dogs rattle their bones
run after taillights of cars perched
on a dirt road lit only by the moon
stars pointing to a gorge where unheard
prayers plunge
if wheels skid & fail to grip.

This much I know.

I like the magic of dandelions you defend against neighbors
when our meadow blooms in June with weeds.

I like to sunbathe
in our backyard with you.

I like silences you recognize & know their names
as if they were stars on a cloudless night.

I like that I was unafraid
to drive on Death Road with you.

This much I know. I want to be
with you on the road with a dead end.

Good Life

May you die
well

in a body
worn out by time

your eyes pain
free & kind

gleaming
with yet another joke.

May the picture
of a woman

who gave you children
be clear

& the grown sons
by your bedside

at ease with shadows
at their feet.

Shadow Puppets

our house grows dark corners
        hinges that rattle
                when doors slam then lock

our marriage
        locked in a holding pattern
                stained by Cabernet

King Crimson
        on full volume
                & suddenly vulgar words

what a shame!—
        hurtful words
                that stain our puppet mouths

words pulling light from
        our startled puppet eyes—
                two spinning stars

in the dark Covid sky

husband & wife

               removed from motherland

sharing lungs & amygdala

thread beads of apologies   they embroider hope   on their skin—

                                                      lovemaking

they hold their breath   create silences   worthy of forgiveness

afraid they will hate more

& never love less   blinding hawks that hunt

                                                    for songbirds

untethered by thoughts

loud fear   rattling like rivets   in their heads

clings to their lips

like a lit Marlboro Red

until its toxic cloud cripples   the bodies they share—

soft spots   tempting   the oceanic creatures

                         to curl upside down

in their chests   between words   that soar & crawl

Failed Assignment

In my story,
I lie about my characters & steal
identities of people I know
who appear plain

& increasingly pitiful

on paper. I need to change them,
make them three-dimensional,
introduce peril, so I make the woman
kiss her man & hiss

"pack your stuff & leave"

then I wonder if he will,
who will keep the house
& tend to the garden, & I decide
she does, but they split

the dogs, dishes, & photos

& shuffle the children
who become unruly
& anxious. In the end
I don't know how to arc this plot

without killing at least one of them.

Older

Sky in my eyes. Grey
clouds with a sliver of moon
for a hairpin.

A fallen oak branch
becomes my bench
by water's edge.

I mistake my reflection
for an enemy, a soaring heron
an apostrophe.

To Aging Well

To praise a cabbage soup, hands
that chopped the leaves & chose
the right amount of fennel seeds.

    To sit on a park bench
    together, sunlight erasing
    shadows from furrowed brows.

        To tell a spouse to put
        down the carried load
        carelessly picked up years ago.

            To wish his former lover
            happiness. To do it
            before leaving.

October

Last year deer decimated
generosa roses in the flower bed by the water.
Well-intentioned friends advised
to plant marigolds. So I did.

This summer a fat groundhog

moved in under a porch next door
& ate the yellow flowers then ruined
the purple echinacea & basil garden.
The only flowers left

are hardy asters. Poison

ivy crawls over the patio & climbs
up my favorite pine tree—
her feathered branches a shelter
for a family of bluebirds. Look!

they are flying away!

Letting Them Go

After the last plastic bin, the last
suitcase & a bundle of sheets,
the last box of books,
a fan, a lamp, the guitar & the last
pair of running shoes
are assigned their new place
on shelves, under beds, & always open
closets on college grounds
where stars and maximum potential
are waiting to be reached,

I return home to reconnect
with an independent woman
inside me. I take the last look
at three empty bedrooms upstairs
where an African drum
already collects dust,
volumes of mysteries
& classic tales
patiently wait
among the soccer & dance trophies
organized at an angle, or randomly
on shelves like a collage
against the backdrop of green, blue, & pink walls,

& I rest on a quilt embroidered with ballerinas.
I sense my children's presence
but cannot hug them,
& I see their faces but cannot
whisk away wisps
of hair falling in their eyes
& suddenly silence
is cut by the shrill
cry of a wounded animal
curled on my daughter's bed.

Slideshow

I have the worry
stone my daughter brought
from a school trip to Ireland.
When my thumb rubs
the smooth indent in the green marble
her thoughtfulness lifts
my thoughts & presses
them down into the stone.

*

My sons rarely ask for company or anything
that could clutter their space.
Are you happy? I ask.

*

The skirt of her red velvet dress
swirls, treetops spin sunlight on her face.
Rocky Road ice cream melts.

*

Sensing the perfect wave
he greets her with a trusting smile
then stabs the water & dives into the surf.

*

The baby asleep in my belly unfolds
her limbs like dawn petals.

*

He stands on the sidewalk by his dorm waving
then leaps at my moving car, knocks on the window
& says "Love you, mom."

*

Like young Icarus winged
with wonder, he paraglides
above garlands of Hida mountains.

*

He reassures me
he has walked foreign lands & does not
fear the unfamiliar.

*

Imprints left on pillows slowly rise
& erase. Children's chatter fades away.

*

A clown sits on the moon
& fishes, a fireball lands
on a yellow brick road,
a sign points to the North Pole,
to the Underworld, to a locked diary,
a silver key taped to its cover.

Doing Dishes with My Son

He loads the dishwasher the way I do:
plates facing the jet stream,
mugs organized by height,
utensils spooning on the upper rack.
He states in his unruffled voice
that my glass of red wine
left half empty
on the counter every night
is a stable feature.
Like a piece of furniture, he jokes.
Then he says good things don't happen
to him. I say, only bad things
simply happen. Everything else
is intention & work.

I tell him to talk kindly to the man
in a mirror, hoping that dimmed eyes
never look back at him.

Visiting My Son in Japan

In Koyasan

      baby swallows await
      their mother, colorful mouths
      open & hungry

In Hiroshima

      the red-crowned crane still
      on the Atomic Dome's ruins
      scarlet petunias in bloom

On Miyajima Island

      a lost fawn cries
      five-storied wooden pagoda
      consoles the souls

In Kyoto

      rows of orange gates
      at dawn, a mystic pathway
      to my son's future

Keeping You Safe

You are where you are
supposed to be, a place you chose
& earned, diploma
above the IKEA desk you trudged
up steep stairs to assemble step-by-step
yourself. Yet, I wish
you were still in college
within a distance I could manage or,
better yet, back in high school
where at every parent-teacher conference
you were praised, & I beamed
knowing where you were heading, except
that morning in November
when the wheels of your Ford slid
on wet leaves steering you into a ditch,
or the time I lost control driving home
with you, & we hung upside down
until police arrived. When I think about it,
I wish you were back in my belly
developing webbed toes, listening
to my heartbeat, eyes fused shut.

Syzygy

Her life would not have been his life
had they said *No* instead of *Yes*.

The children wouldn't be

hers or his.   Imagine.

They wouldn't be.

There is sun

there is moon

& there is earth where life unfolds.

They can't exist without each other
but rarely do they align.

When they do   it's spectacular.

Part Three

At a House Party

most employ humor
to say the unsayable

jokes the epicenter of every exchange
laughter like torture for hours

my mouth stuffed
with metaphors picking at my bones

glass eyes
in a stupid stare

our ridiculous world

on honeysuckle twines
hummingbirds   don't hum

red-bellied woodpeckers
don't drum on car mirrors

& damselflies stop hovering
in mid-air   we all are

spinning into madness
          & something escapes

through the tunnels of our eyes
cells mutate & multiply

attack   & hijack the breath

Covid-19 Guilt Poem

we are guilty of
faking orgasms
confidence & composure

flat stomach
& an upbeat state of
mind—on an inhale

occasional syncope
episode on a kitchen floor
& arguments over crumbs—

our minds shaped
oddly like jigsaw puzzles
stained by wine

guilty of binging
on CNN
coffee & *The Crown*

decades old friendships
dumped over QAnon
conspiracies

our children
the nucleus
we are guilty of arresting—

lines to food banks
& vaccine sites like ant colonies
miles long

Global Change

A hybrid tree in Pennsylvania
grows lavish Asian pears while labs breed
red-fleshed apples.

A river quits her job
of flowing & confuses
wild salmon which carry their loads across

but the shore has recently moved
to a place without an address.
It might be eco-camping

on the bottom of the Amazonian basin
where piranhas lose their teeth chewing
on the water sediments

& threatened tribes dye
their skin red with annatto seeds, shooting
arrows at low-flying planes.

Chernobyl, 26 April 1986

Winds blew North for three days,
skies were blue & clear, the air
smelled of cherry & magnolia,

radiation spreading
from a little Ukrainian town
over wheat & rye fields

in Belarus & Poland,
crossing the Baltic Sea, reaching
rich Sweden & Norway.

Radiation fell gently
on buds of growing grains,
on blossoms of pear & apple trees,

into rapid river waters
where cows lined up
to drink, kids waded

in shallow ponds while mothers
washed clothes with soapstone.
Warm wind carrying the ionizing

atoms sneaked into homes
through windows left ajar.
Spring was in the air.

The Aftermath

we didn't see the nuclear blast,
didn't have to flee
our block apartments
leaving pots of beet soup boiling,
TVs with an episode of *Polskie Drogi* on,
we did not smell the petrified burning
but the air fragrant with lilac

above our homes – radiation
settling in our bones,
hijacking embryos,
cancerous cells now bright
on MRIs like the Milky Way
on a cloudless night.

Enigma of Distance

The train leaves the Central Station,
glides past yellow green
checkerboards of rye & wheat.

When it comes to a halt,
armed soldiers guard
every entry, German Shepherds sniff
steps nobody climbs.

Conductors whistle then close doors.
Through lowered windows
smoke from unfiltered cigarettes
escapes over a wall
strung with barbed wire.

It was a 24-hour train ride
in '81 from Warsaw to Paris
but distance isn't a straight line
time can measure. The Wall
in Berlin has fallen—

the wall south of the U.S. border
is high & painted black, its steel plates
designed to burn & cut.

"Guernica"

the incandescent lamp   in the eye of the sun
burns
fear-draped backs   on a dirt road

         ironclad law
         separates
         families

a helicopter whirls   over a cornfield

         the open palm
         of a pecan tree
         holds   a song

the bull s
      k
        y
           dives
so dark of himself
he thinks jingoism   has wings

alternate reality

on all channels. an elephant

at a telescope. a donkey
removes a cap from the lens

(a good servant it is).
the act of servitude confuses

the elephant. his penis
brain a copper penny.

during pandemic he wears
a face of a flattened toad

emptied of empathy. he masks
his shortcomings with money

& unearths combat instincts
in all of us. reality with

a screw so loose it barely holds.

Negotiation

take television   football
games & presidential debates

take ill-fitting dresses   fashion
necklaces & guns

take detours   ruling against abortion
dead-ends & shallow all

take leaf blowers & lawn mowers
(but leave the leaves & lawns)

you can take gluten-free bagels
boxed white wine & amazon prime

but leave grapevine plantations
& golden fields of wheat & rye

leave the wind raking cloudy sky
& dandelions growing dismay

leave the ebbing & pulling oceans
a silver moon & constellations of

choices like a river on a summer's eve
like a Northern Star   holding still

In the melting pot

of lowlands & mountains
a divide   a mile deep

on the south a steel wall
twenty feet high

on the east windows
boarded up against looters

& on the west trees
burn for weeks

constant blood   moon against
shrouds of smoke that choke

like the knee
          on a neck

Northern New Jersey Town

Ghosts live in this town that sits
cross-legged by the border of two states.

One ghost bought a pothole
at the corner of a dead-end road.
He's a drummer who plays with the wind.

Another ghost is an engraved word
& sits upon his tomb overlooking a pond
where a pair of swans mates.

Another, a sky wanderer, is a rain
cloud shaped like corn flour
milled from an uprooted oak.

One ghost lost his feet
while sleeping. The hungover dawn
didn't wake him.

After the ghost of Blue Man Rock
didn't catch a falling heron,
its bones spun the moon.

These ghosts climb cliffs
sharp like tongues
grinding their stories with iron claws.

They also like to hang
upside down over mown lawns
seeded with elephants & flags.

One ghost's favorite ghost
is his shadow & it follows him home
like the squirrels he eats.

Semester Abroad in India

When Skype rings, I trace on the screen
my daughter's face, smooth
out her pink hair pulled back in a braid.

She cannot say she's been happy
if happiness is lack
of stress or worry.

There are many kinds of happiness
I say, mostly moments.
She agrees. Meditating in an ashram

or dancing in the Celebration of Lights
is bliss but how does one
give life meaning, she asks.——

In Jodhpur, where fifteen thousand
Pakistani refugees live, she learns Hindi,
records the words of men with weathered eyes.

Imprinted in dirt of the Thar Desert
for miles, their stories
finally leave the Blue City.

book of faces

i log in to read
updates on my children

liking their comments
hearting their photos

scrolling
through posts

of friends i haven't met
face to face

yet i know
their daily diet

whom they vote for
& how they feel

about lady gaga's mic drop
at half-time

while newsfeed's
phonemes & graphemes

stored in the cloud
poke & obscure

Cosmic Rules

There is the Sun
    & other massive
        stars smaller than
            thumbnails.

What interests us
is a planet abundant in water & trees
    with its own
        orbiting moon

where night
twists people
inside their heads—their lives
in horizontal chaos.

There is
    a mountain
& at its foot
    a man
on his knees.

Struck

To Sylvia & Rachel

Bees stop buzzing on purple hydrangea.
A butterfly stops waltzing on purple azalea

& quiets the flutter of wings in the wind.

When do we quiet the flutter of longing?
A stag leaps off a cliff. Escaping hunting dogs

a stag jumps off a cliff.
He dives gently into the earth's throat

when out of the blue, heartache strikes.

the unknown

someone is born & someone
is already unremembered
but doesn't know it as I write this line.

by the time I finish the stanza
two hundred sixty people will be born
one hundred eight will die.

by now that number has already changed
so has the sky. look!
raindrops arc the violet light.

Storm

We enter unknown spaces
give names to clouds
stars & children.

Drawn to faraway places

we stir the skies.
We are unburdened by
memories—

we think we have time.

No longer young
we mend & revise
& love as if in revenge

for all things that went wrong.

Tattoos

on skin's soft canvas
a needle embroiders
directions for living

dispersed

petals of a flower
inevitably wilting
the way names do

circling
in black ink
the inside of an arm

to be deciphered
on a deathbed
like hieroglyphs

Thesaurus

Some words are black holes
some pull like a sunlit moon

Some words like paper
lanterns burn & collapse

Some are weights
waiting to be unchained

Some words drip at a low dose
settling in the sacrum

Some scratch the throat or soothe
like honey drops

Some words knot the intestines
or puncture the lung

Some words stay behind
a double fence of teeth

Some words are never said

Ars Poetica Triptych

the cobblestone past
bleeds through her fingertips   nights attract werewolves
                                                       & other strange things
                                                       like unicorns and prayer
silence steeps   in her head

                            she stays
resistant to logic   but take a closer look   keys to her subconscious
                                                       compose her intentions
diamond assumptions
& word conspiracies   under the soft roof
of her mouth

                        foreign sounds
                        on linked strands
                        roll into the inked lines
she doesn't write
in long sentences   with correctly placed pauses
                    making sense.

Acknowledgments

I am grateful that Stephen F. Austin State University Press has provided a home for my poems. Special thanks to Mallory LeCroy for her help in the publication process.

Grateful acknowledgment is made to the editors of the following publications where some of the poems in this book, sometimes in a different form, first appeared:

The American Journal of Poetry: "Homepage"
Border Crossing: "The Other Side"
CALYX: "To a Foreign Language" (part of an essay)
Fibreview: "Fibonacci Spiral"
Glassworks: "In the melting pot," "Failed Assignment"
Literary Mama: "I Named Her Nina"
Lumina: "My Mother's Necklace"
NarrativeNortheast: "Older," "A Woman"
Paterson Literary Review: "Doing Dishes with My Son," "Remembrance," "With You"
Poets Reading the News: "Guernica"
Shot Glass Journal: "Curse," "the day the light went out," "Tattoos," "Tidal Wave," "To Aging Well"
The Stillwater Review: "Visiting My Son in Japan"
Survision: "Insomnia," "Northern New Jersey Town"
Tipton Poetry Journal: "Cosmic Rules"
Waxing & Waning: "Shadow Puppets" (part of an essay)

Thank you to Finishing Line Press for embracing my early work and publishing chapbooks *Stories Her Hands Tell* & *Here and There* where earlier versions of these poems first appeared: "Seven Years of Plenty," "Weekend at Wyndham Hotel," "Like a Loving Mother" & "Balicka Street, 1981," "What Flows in Our Veins," "Kids & Fish Have No Voice," "our ridiculous world," & "Chernobyl, 26 April 1986," respectively.

My sincere gratitude to teachers & poets: Timothy Liu, John Parras, & Christopher Salerno for their guidance, wisdom, & encouragement. Special thanks to my fellow poets from a Ringwood poetry group: Anna Appel, Katia Arco, Mary Crosby, Alan Fedeli, Jeanne Fleming, Karen Lee Ramos, Joan Page-Durante, Joan Saunders, Val Schermerhorn, & Julie Wells for their insights & advice.

Separate thanks to my parents, Ludmiła & Zygmunt Ryznar, & my sisters, Monika & Milena, for always finding time to read & comment on my poems.

Finally, my heartfelt gratitude to my husband, Peter, for his unwavering support, my sons, Sebastian & Kristian, & my daughter, Karina, for their inspirations & love. Thank you for all the notebooks with thoughtful dedications.

Special thanks to Karina for creating the beautiful paintings for this book's cover.

EDYTTA ANNA WOJNAR, born and raised in Poland, now lives with her husband in northern New Jersey, where she teaches at William Paterson University. She is the author of two chapbooks: Stories Her Hands Tell (2013) and Here and There (2014) published by Finishing Line Press. Her poems have appeared in The American Journal of Poetry, Border Crossing, Lumina, Narrative Northeast, and Paterson Literary Review, among others. Her creative non-fiction was published or is forthcoming in *Cagibi*, *CALYX*, *Ponder Review*, and *Waxing & Waning*.

CPSIA information can be obtained
at www.ICGtesting.com
Printed in the USA
LVHW090521190322
713645LV00006B/18